Sound Check
A Musician's Journey in Song and Verse

Copyright © 2017
Elisa Grajeda-Urmston
Tamara Adams
ISBN: **978-0-9912975-8-0**
Published by Jamii Publishing
San Bernardino, CA
www.JamiiPublishing.com

All rights reserved.

For every girl who ever played a guitar…

Sound Check
A Musician's Journey in Song and Verse

Elisa Grajeda-Urmston
Tamara Adams

Set List:

1)
La Sirena…..5
After the Midnight Screening at the Strand…..6
The Eleventy-Seven Anxieties of Being on the Road…..7
Chickie's Brilliant Career…..8
Yesenia…..9
Drowned Out by Road Noise…..11
Do the Math…..12
Girl Meets Coyote Outside Tuba City at Midnight…..13
Songbird's Jungle…..15

2)
The Red Hen…..20
Laurel Canyon…..22
Ashes and Tears…..23
What Happens in Vegas…..24
La Sirena Sings…..25
Doheney…..27
Glimmer…..29

3)
Consumed…34
One Percent…..35
In an Orange County Bar…..37
Grady…..38
Chick Singer Daydreaming Between the Notes of a Song….. 39
Romance…..40
Song for the Ex…..41

4)
Nidal…..46
Notes…..47

Thank you…..55
About the Author/About the Artist…..59

Set 1

La Sirena

Here in
this sea of
smiles, hips
and breasts
I ride the
musical current of scales
and guitar strings, lay myself
bare before you with love songs
sing seduction over small talk
and bar room brawls
smoke and clatter
lure lines
dollar shots
and sexy chatter
I'm here singing to you
embracing that microphone
with deep funky midnight blues
cumbia and hip-hop too, played
to pluck you from that drink
so I hope it wasn't my song
that made you become
the Sig-alert I passed
as I drove home
in the LA rain
alone, my
love
one early
Saturday morning after
Last   call

After the Midnight Screening at the Strand

Ocean Beach pier late fog chill
sodium streetlight pierces starless black…
& bathes us yellow and veinless in it's glare
by the rusted VW, flat tire, no spare

Out past curfew, Coronado Avenue mostly hushed and still
graffiti and empty beer bottles mark the trail back
echoes of biker bar jukebox rumble, smoke & Wind Song perfume
a path of sand covered asphalt caressed by fuchsia iceplant blooms

Huddled by the fire pit, in the post-buzz gloom,
she'll— on a beater guitar, play Landslide--Fleetwood Mac
while he lights up that sweet hash from Marrakech
forbidden hour, waves crash, goose bump flesh

Before the dawn patrol surfers show
but long after the panhandlers have left

The Eleventy-Seven Anxieties of Being on the Road

There is no how-to guide for how to prepare for a month on the road. I have managed to learn this much: You clean the house, knowing when you get home, spiders will still have moved into your bed. Pack. It helps to make a list. Use up all perishables. Cook yourself a tortilla over an open burner; char it around the edges just a little, the way Abuelita does. You won't be able to get food like this in the casino. Savor it. Say goodbye to your friends. Stop the mail delivery. Turn off the stove. Realize that no matter how many times you check that stove before leaving, you will find yourself in a cold-sweat panic somewhere along Nevada SR3, certain that you left it on. Remind yourself when that happens, that you are closer to Winnemucca than home, and so, well, so be it. Sneak out before dawn, so as to avoid saying goodbye to los abuelos who live next door. As much as they hate you leaving to go anywhere, they hate it even more that you became a musician, even though they paid for your guitar lessons. "Gypsy," they call you—and you're not sure they mean the kind that stole Abuelito's wallet in France, or the burlesque stripper. Suspect they like that ambiguity. Ni modo. The last time you left, Abuelito only said, "When I die, cremate me. I don't want them digging me up like los momias en Guanajuato someday." Make a mental note of how swollen his ankles are these days. He is dying. But you have to make a living. Remind yourself there is nothing selfish about that; people take business trips every day, and that's what this is. Pull into the truck stop in Tonopah; use the restroom there, because experience has taught you it's one of the less frightening ones you'll come across. While you're at it, buy Snowballs and a dusty bag of Doritos. Hit the road again. Eat compulsively to swallow the guilt. Turn the radio up to drown out the echo of Abuelita's comment that only prostitutes and Liberace wear rhinestones and, pues, you don't play piano. Somewhere past Fallon, notice the herd of wild mustangs running in the pink sunset, and how that same sun hitting your rhinestone jacket fills the cab of your truck with a million little iridescent stars, and realize you really did leave the stove on. Wonder if this is the time you will come home to ashes

Chickie's Brilliant Career

He says only loose birds sing
buys her apology Lalique
and a ring to clip her wings
     she refuses to answer him,
     knows he likes them meek and
     is only interested in nesting, settling
     but some birds prefer six strings to a ring

…and know only dust reconciles and settles burying
     every shiny thing; a home, a cage, a coop, a tomb
     feathered with static silver crystal and icey gems

              Twisted visions rock his leery mind he
              dreams of the well-mannered strain &
                traces her facial features as a threat a
              menacing caress after evening's crystal
              leaded highball and 18 year -old scotch

            her walls close in, options spin, so damned
        tired of eggshell walks and finding fault, flies —
and returns to what always mattered to her most:

In a pawnshop flip, wary, hurried, a nervous bitten lip
she buys that six-stringed blue Telecaster axe, & at
the bus station ticket window, a one-way trip
Knowing no turning back, singing though
glistening shards remain as the scars
of blind fury and freedom flight
feathers   bloodied but
bars behind her.

Yesenia

I remember when you first learned to make yourself invisible The wind told me:
eventually you might fly
Back then, it used to tell me everything
but I chose not to believe it that day
We were so close I knew how you felt by the sound of your breath
so you wouldn't leave me
how could you?
But
looking back, I see
mere flight was never good enough for you
No, instead
you practiced the art of disappearance
dark sorcery with bad boys and magic powders
so clumsily at first
things got broken
First, mere possessions
a cup
a stove
But that day you made an entire car vanish
I should have known right then you were on your way
All I heard the night you got it right
was a breeze
a stirring of leaves
and a wind chime clattering to the ground
The Princess of Broken Things hushed
the nightbirds and coyotes and the neighborhood dogs
as she closed the door
not bothering to look back
Half awake, I thought I saw
La Llorona dancing naked in the moonlight
whispering, "everything, everything…"
so I didn't say goodbye to you, surely
you must know that
In your absence
you are here
more than you ever were--
The way a chill on a balmy night carries
the scent of your hair or
how I catch my breath when I see you in every woman I meet

and how everything
everything
is in the wind

Drowned Out By Road Noise

The hurtful word, things said but unheard
buzzing like a hummingbird wing or
a worn guitar string that, upon unraveling
leaves the whole instrument out of tune
And we were traveling again
leaving Taos that day
chased by a late spring storm that menaced us
all the way down the
Sangre de Cristos, you
staring down the broken line
as I traced the mermaid on my Starbucks cup
Faded asphalt glinting lighter than the steel wool sky
road noise whine, a caution sign ignored
In your head a lightning flash
tapping your fingers on the wheel
to some unheard Merle Haggard song
he always did sing the best songs about restlessness
and moving on, better than Willie, Cash or Jones
And we were creatures of the road, after all
You turned to me somewhere
outside Bernalillo while
our gear rattled the rhythm of Highway 25
in that old truck bed like
a drummer with timing issues
drowning out the subtlety of your assertion that
it was always like me to play one song too many

But You Were A Redhead Then, So Do the Math...

                It's so
                easy
                to
                lose
                track
                of
                days
                'cause
                you
                measure
                them
                by
                when
                your
                strings
                go
                dead

When your day at the office is a
night in a bar, just how many string changes
equal a year? You measure those by dive bars,
different hair colors, strange towns new guitars,
and this-is-the-one romances that fill your
lame little fishbowl world, then disappear
leaving you gutted and butterflied,
all but consumed until all you can
really lay claim to is a lifetime of calendars
marked in club dates, net figures and agent numbers
the inventory of your so-called shortcomings, guitar picks
worn thin and empty perfume bottles, note how it is the sweet
scent still lingers like a past sweetheart's warm morning bed and
fill that hunger with diet pills, a chaser of Cuervo Gold lime&salt
followed by the after-gig breakfasts that burn heavy as you
drive home, blinded by the sunrise & last night's regrets
ringing like an unstoppable feedback in your head
What was that song again — tell me please?

Girl Meets Coyote at Midnight, Outside Tuba City (With Apologies to Robert Johnson)

El Accordion from a Norteña song
competes for the same
airwave as a pedal-steel guitar while border
crossings and billboard signs fly
past my window. Beyond Winslow, a coyote strides across the road
tossing me a sly glance, a canine flick of a tail

Then, temporarily forgotten like a drunkard's tale
the vanishing mirage leaves me to the business, the hoary song
of racing to see what goes first, my rodehard
looks or my sense of humor, flying past this same
dream scene: the audience of a kit fox in the creosote bush, the bottlefly
electric buzz and the silence of rattlesnakes and stars, what borders

on phobia, it finds me stranded at the crossroads, a border
town in some dust mote desert place, lined face, a nightmare fairytale,
it plays a siren song perverting reality; me? Honey, strictly fly
by night, an ambulance wail that jars sleep, yet its dissonant distant song,
its siren call, lures and lulls with the whoosh of passing cars, but the same
song screams in midnight dingy dive bars where sanity erodes

and my only sun is a blaze of cobweb faded end-of-the-road
dumps burnt-out stage lights, trip over boarded up venues, a boarder
in my own life, crashed on the rocks, the crumbling echoes of that same
stale performance every night- Coyote trickster's tale
let me flail, or leave me to listen to that old song
a warning my ancestors and past loves sang, voices droning like flies

in my head, like ghosts chanting from Window Rock, time flies,
M'ija, while radio waves oscillate & fade, the road
howls like a theremin whine, a siren call, a coyote-lonely song
tells me I'm moving on going nowhere crossing that border
from sexy to hag too fast, in this pitiful tale
old as time. Better turn that radio dial, baby, better find a new game

'cause right now, every town—every stage— feels the same
every night, and whether I drive or fly
I arrive, and live this recurring tale
of a rubato, out –of-meter life on the road
a disembodied existence both minstrel and vagabond that borders
on sounding like the trite lyrics of a honkytonk song—

a song that is, every night, the same
bordering on flight (though not quite)
this roadweary siren's tale

Songbird's Jungle

Hotel
facade
washed in
halogen light
glossy bird
of
paradise
paints a sterile Rousseau scene of
shiny postcard palms and glowing purple
orchids untouched by blight and bugs
a lobby glass unsmudged
the reflection startles
her into flight
a freight elevator
so the guests never see her
ascension in grimy steel diamond
plate boxes or traverse the Byzantine
back corridors to the magenta and
blue smoke-filled stage where the
drumbeats carry a message of
Techno joy and menace
Songbird, gardenia
behind her ear
low-cut to there
at her high heels
wires coil & writhe
and snap venomous
at her ankles she flies
over mic-line vines
black tendrils coil & snare
She knows to keep moving
the jungle reclaims every still thing eventually.

Set 2

The Red Hen

When I was twelve
my mom took my sister and me to the Del Mar fair
I know we probably rode the rides
looked at the sheep and cows and things
and ate the hot dogs and corn on the cob on a stick
and cotton candy
because that's pretty much what we did every time we went to the fair
I'm thinking my sister was in a dance recital there
She was always the graceful one
The Pretty One—
the one who would go places
It was more than likely the main reason we went
since my mom never was a big fan of carnival rides, livestock, or hot dogs
The cotton candy, only maybe
But honestly, the only thing I really remember about that day
was a live, copper-colored hen in a small Plexiglas box on wheels
the box stood fairly high
like an old-fashioned popcorn machine
so the bird was more or less at eye-level
She was alone in there, save for a toy piano
If you put a quarter in the slot, the chicken would play a song
on the piano
Mary Had a Little Lamb
and for that, a few kernels of dried corn would be dispensed into the box
and the chicken would then scurry around and eat them
I remember being amazed that she could actually play a recognizable tune
I also felt sorry for her
What if she wasn't in the mood?
Did the throng of people around the box scare her?
Was she lonely in there?

I remember asking my mama all these questions
and probably more
on the car ride home until she finally snapped that
the chicken was better off than most people
that the chicken didn't have a big enough brain to be bothered
by these things
that the chicken's "talent" would at least keep it from being eaten, anyway
and that it was only a chicken in a box, for Pete's sake, &

that she didn't want to hear another word about the damned thing anymore
and how she regretted ever showing it to me in the first place
and to just be quiet, already

Average Pay for a Southern California Bar band:
$500/Night, divided between however many are in the band. Sometimes, bands offer female vocalists "skinny pay," because they are not considered a "real" part of the band

Laurel Canyon

Recurrent dream turquoise pools
filters hum punctuated by wild parrots
singing car alarm songs
Peacocks and Porsches
Lives carved out in the
wild sumac, hillsides of bouganville
and iceplant psychedelia fallen
jacaranda blossoms cling to my skin
as I swim and the
radio purrs an Eagles song
One of These Nights
coyotes yip kit fox scream in the distance as
this Angel lays herself at my feet,
No gold dust woman, no lady of the canyon, no.
All eyes are on her—
Hollow and shiny
ringing and buzzing
humming like a resonator guitar
a high-maintenance woman cloaked
in June gloom, kept
sweet, cool, cashmere grey seduction
either way, you dare not look away
lest the Santa Anas give birth to flames
that consume us
fill our mouths with ashes

Ashes and Tears

Sweet-faced southern boy
from Mount Olive, Waycross or Tupelo
You come to us
with your gigbag full of demons
and a million dollar dream
rhinestone suit & that devil tuned
Silvertone guitar
Is there something in the cypress breeze
A melancholy conveyed in a magnolia blossom
or sand pine's sigh
that only you can sense
Bitter pill
New Year's Day in Knoxville
Hunkered down in Graceland
Burning in the starlit desert night
Sadness bigger than a song

What Happens in Vegas

She's just one
of the boys
Guitar slung low
Herein a town
where you crawl
on the
shards of
every broken dream that ever
rattled down the strip to die Shhhh.
Stop. Be really quiet: can you feel the suicides
in the hotel rooms the nightmares in the back-alleys
like an itchy sweater on your skin? Listen: don't
exhale Step on that Scale, cause everyone knows
a woman's worth in this town that
tight little template
the cut of a surgeon's knife
and a bottle of bleach Leave your
intellect at the city limit sign. It'll only
hurt you here gazing out from your room
the view the bare-bottom billboards and the
casinos the liquor joint on Charleston Avenue
porn pamphlet sidewalk confetti littered streets
Hear the showgirl, singer, waitress, cashier maid
each screaming, "I am" with her smile
above the jingling pinging machines,
clattering chips, and murmuring
crowd buzzing like a bad
guitar pickup or
neon ants in her veins
the entertainment
director's dilemma:
what to do with that chick
that thing with the guitar She
don't   look   like much,   Wow but
Man, she   sure can play

La Sirena Sings

Yes, but you 'play' for a living,
my sister famously pointed out once.
Wrong. For the record, I don't play.
I'm not playing when I creep into casinos
in the middle of the night
through the back service entrances
past the dumpsters and cockroaches
the sullen, faceless loading-dock workers in rubber boots
who make sure I know how much I am inconveniencing them by
just being there
I am not playing when I blow into town like a ghost
bleary-eyed, road-weary and grimy
introduce myself to the house sound engineer
who invariably looks right through me as we shake hands
set up my gear behind ratty velvet curtains
and later, perform silly songs for people who really don't give a hang and
I do that in four-inch heels while wearing a smile
then tear it all down and move on
to the next nightclub
the next casino, the next town
the next oasis of bright lights
And I'm not playing when I drive hundreds of miles
across the Nevada desert
past mountains
the running herds of wild mustangs
the miles of dilapidated barbed wire fence remnants
making pit stops in little towns that time has forgotten
before speeding on again to the next sound-check
the next beacon of lights
praying the mile markers like a rosary
being everywhere and nowhere
Everywhere and nowhere,
a modern-day migrant worker
In high heels and a rhinestone jacket
and a truck full of speakers, guitars
wires and synthesizers
following the crops of fame or notoriety
as aimlessly but sure as smoke
rising to meet the jewel-toned stage lights
success measured not by how much I pick, but
by seeing my name up in the glare

of some garish casino marquis—
Pioche, Tonopah, Winnemucca:
the only reason I know I wasn't dreaming
when I passed through these places
is that I've bought gas in all of them
I never buy gas in my dreams
        Only in life

Doheny, 1973

I loiter the sidewalk between Sunset and Santa Monica
high from the exhaust fumes of the traffic jam, the
flirtations of the people passing on the street
sharing the same air as songwriters
making change-the-world music
The jangle of that sound pours
from car radios, boutiques and nightclub doors
Honking horns and motorcycle roars
neon and billboards
twelve string Rics, turquoise, tie-dye
incense and patchouli
Music that's a chemical, a pheromone
a love potion of sound
We meet at the Troubadour
surreal and real you, golden guitar man sweet you
Slip out the backstage door
& In your Jag,
go silently cruising through
neighborhoods of mansions and Spanish-style bungalows
Low, full moon strobing
through the palm trees of Beverly Boulevard
whipping through the enchanted forest
of pepper trees and eucalyptus that hugs
the curves of Mullholland
From the overlook
the shimmering grid of the Valley crouches
air heavy with the scent of
laurel sumac, canyon yarrow, purple nightshade
You, silky hair in my face
whispering pleading, loving words I can't make out
After
you use your shirt
to dry the fog from the windshield
A solitary chaser of pills, morphine and Jack,
still unzipped, you drive me home,
kisses but no numbers exchanged
leaving me to dream you every day:
your lips on my cheek, that trail of dark down below your navel
the hollow below your Adam's apple
the way your long hair was scented musk and tobacco
and how you trembled as my fingers

brushed the nape of your neck,
the rhythm of our hips and sighs —
things nobody knows from your glossy promo shot
smiling out from that Rolling Stone obituary.

Glimmer

The gaze from the stage
A flirt that fuels the force
Proves too much for the girl who should know
The danger of currents
Rip tides and
voltage when wet
Driven by Wattage
And every word to every one of his songs
Brimming with masculine malevolence
Confection or confession
Is a charge
That sets off an arrhythmia
In a sea of willing victims
Somewhere in the walls, a wire sparks and flames
Come sunrise in the
coastal mist, thigh bruised by a kiss
From a rumpled bed she hears a single dove
beyond her balcony window
Singing backup vocals
Sympathy for the Devil

Set 3

Consumed

Sometimes I just need a change of scene when it's all too much
she says, while freewheeling down Pearblossom Highway
west, past everything familiar, sound and touch

Past tracts and valleys, citrus groves, the display
of strawberry crops and shopping malls that become some
somnambulant So-Cal dream that creeps like jimsonweed, green-grey

Wild, invasive, narcotic, rendered numb
until only her mirror reminds her of what she should already know:
objects are larger than they appear, exhausted from

A rip-current pull, relentless, released from the flow
somewhere between Anacapa and State because
past whitewashed walls swallowed by flowering vines' magenta glow

Pride of Madeira in full bloom, sounds of coffee house froth & buzz
beach town jangle, the restaurants full of sun-kissed people on cellphones
a homeless guy dumpster diving for food who was

behind the corporate flagship store, the no parking zones
beyond all this florid static, the hunger calls—
for her, it's nothing new, it always will, it owns

her—primordial, certain; the sea cliff walls
plane of pewter shimmer, pelican swoon,
dolphins feed, seaweed tangle falls

She's come again looking for shells, abalone-cowrie-moon
washed up, pretty things or
something hard to wrap herself in against grey coastal June

gloom or worse, maybe a little of both— more
of a warning or a comfort, a solace or a curse, hold it close,
hear how it sings for

her, time slows
stops, stop. Stay.
Remember this place, and the song only she knows

One Percent of What Rattles Around in the Chick Singer's Head...

Chord charts
Lyrics
Agents' phone numbers
The faces of friends you haven't seen in months
It isn't personal
The driving distance between Las Vegas and Reno, Winnemucca to Wendover
The band house will always suck. Travel with Lysol and your own pillow
Don't eat the turkey in the EDR of the Golden Nugget, but they have a Froot Loop dispenser
that's pretty cool
They don't really like California bands in Phoenix
The truck stop outside Gallup has okay food and clean bathrooms
The graveyard shift in Wendover...again
It isn't personal
Price minus the 15% agent's fee nets you...
Tear down in Tucson at 2:00 a.m., sound check in Albuquerque the next day at noon
Who did you piss off in your last life to deserve this?
I hope you enjoyed it
Agents are the devil, it isn't personal
Repeat after me: the soundman is God. Repeat it until you believe it. No. Really.
If you wear your belt buckle straight on, you'll scratch up
the back of your guitar
Drummers are always weird, guitar players tend to be ...players, keyboard players are
inevitably control freaks
The time a keyboard player actually handed you a chart for Brick House—all two chords of it
Never play a gig for the exposure; people die from exposure
You should have been there when your uncle passed away
You should have been there for Christmas/Thanksgiving/His graduation/Her birthday/Their
wedding/Your life/don't you dare cry
It isn't personal
The things that get lost on the road: boyfriends, friends, sunglasses, guitars...time...but
Everything is somewhere

Where did that woman get that fabulous dress? And I want her boots
Does this mascara smell like it's gone bad to you?
If you wear your watch on the inside of your wrist, you can discretely check the time as you
play without making the audience think you're bored
The ticking of your biological clock
The gig in Sierra Vista, where you decided sobriety might be overrated
The expiration date stamped somewhere on your forehead
Chickens and Bears and Froot Loops in plexiglass boxes
That guy flirting with you?
It isn't personal
The weird stuff drunks choose to tell you sometimes. Lest you think I go home with pocketfuls
of phone numbers scribbled on bar napkins, no. I go home knowing 1% of the static you see
on a TV is a remnant of the Big Bang, because a drunk astrophysicist told me so one night at a
Denim and Diamonds in Albuquerque. I looked it up.
It's true. They think.
   Everything is somewhere. You should have been there. It isn't personal.

In An Orange County Bar

I
Play guitar
from downbeat to last call
Perfect smiles and party dresses
crowd the dance floor And
again the ritual of the
lonely
plays out while I play on
Almost Mexican me this circus
freak with my God-given talent
God-given breasts and God-
given face in
a sea of spray tanned
Botox and Silicon Barbielandia
Confusing my pulse with the straight
eight beat my heart stopping with the end
of each song I don't know where I begin
and they leave off but I am okay
as long as I'm nothing but time
signature   and   melody
and all I have to feel
is the beat
It's no-tell motel time
the   bouncer   shouts
you don't have to go home, but you can't
stay   here

Grady (Sometimes the Devil Drives a Chevy)

He came to the band looking like our saving grace on his white horse of a ratty-assed $500 Chevy truck, his $2500 custom-made bass in the back. That truck quit running one day after he poured water into the carburetor to "clean" it, and when that caused it to quit running, he never fixed it. He just left it along the side of the road somewhere. We never saw it again. He had a pregnant wife who always looked hollow-eyed and sad, as she would sit, smoking and drinking and watching him perform, and a girlfriend, a pleasant, bunny-faced girl with the apparent IQ of a mollusk, and the rest of us were baffled as to how he could get one woman, let alone two; though to be fair, Grady could sport an undeniable charm when he wanted to. Still, Grady reeked of cheap menthol cigarettes and otherwise smelled like people usually do when they've spent three days in jail. Made it just Hell to carpool with him, that's for sure. Random things went missing when he was around— money, jackets, jewelry, weed... Nobody knew where he came from, and he didn't talk about it. If you asked him about "back home," he'd just clam up. He had no ID. He had no money, no matter how much we paid him. He drank. A lot. Then there was the night he became a human speed bump in a casino parking lot, when the cops accidentally ran over him, and that's not even the day he died; shot in the head by some jealous man whose lover Grady had become involved with, coming to his final rest at the base of a twelve-foot-tall, blood-and-brain-splattered Plexiglas case that was studded around the base with silver dollars and that housed a real stuffed polar bear in Stockman's Casino in Elko, but those are stories for another day

Chick Singer Daydreaming Between the Notes of a Song (Mortality Bites)

And you're standing there on the stage thinking /about all the luck you've had, how many times you could have really fucked it up/ but no, you have more lives than a piebald cat/ you should have woken up dead on more than one occasion/ because even Evel Knievel broke every bone in his body at least once/ and the leaps you made would scare even him/ and you did it in suede platform boots and a mini skirt and a yard of purple hair/ which you can't wear anymore lest you be labeled mutton-dressed-as-lamb/ lest you be labeled crazy/ …crazy: your stalker still sends you email telling you how he'd love to kill you/ and your man just shrugs at that and asks if you really expect him to get into a fight with another man over you/ maybe it's not too late to run away/ and perhaps it made sense to run away and join a rock and roll band when you were sixteen/ and date only men who should have had "Jerk" tattooed on their forehead/ and couldn't they pass a law that allows that after so many complaints, oh…ten, maybe?/ but you're a sucker for a sad story and an easy smile/ a sucker for rabid strays/ plucking the stray greys/ and yet, here you are, alive/ and grinning at your futureless future/ smiling because to do anything less would just be plain rude/ smiling because, like Mrs. Knight used to say, you just aren't dressed without your smile/ and you would like to bite somebody right about now/ but well, that would be rude too—although you could probably do that and keep smiling/ and would that be rude then?/ and how on earth did you live to be thirty/ let alone fifty/ amazed you're still working because you sure as hell ain't cute anymore/ but you're too big to haul 'round back and drown.

Romance

Mocked by the monitor's squeal
recalcitrant fingers on dead strings
mangled solos,
stood up by lyrics that promised to be there
jaded audience, sullen bandmates
& The insecurities swirl
like casino smoke
stench that clings
to hair, to clothes,
then follows me to the parking lot
stalks me on my drive home, its
clammy hand on my thigh
fingering my throat
whispering in my ear, as it dogs me
down the hall and to my bed
like a lover

Little Song in my Head for The Ex (Too Damned Small)

Am7   Bm7
I'll bet you thought I would roam the countryside forever
Am7   Bm7
crying like La Llorona's ghost, ooh…
C#maj7
the day you let me go, never
Bm7
Baby, no—oh, not that bad
C#maj7
"cause I'm a rainbow and only one of my colors is sad
Am7   C#maj7
But damn, how I hate running into you
Am7   C#maj7
at the Miracle Street Laundromat
Am7
or the mall
Bm7   C#maj7
no lipstick, nappy hair, feeling fat
Am7   Bm7
sensing myself aging in dog-years and
Am7   Bm7
cursing my luck for living in a world that's way too small
C#maj7   Am7
La, la, la…

Set 4

Nidal

Woven through the static
the certainty of longitudinal migration
an encoded secret
that defies logic
bucks the slipstream
of fluttered wing
and brings me back to you

Notes From the Chick Singer/The Memo Amended 5/31

Dear band members: I love you all like you're normal, but some things have been brought to my attention that need to be dealt with. Hence this memo.

1) From here on out, no leaning on the wall during a performance, acting like the gig is the most whack thing you have ever done. If you are that tired or displeased, stay home. I work in 4-6 inch heels every night, and have yet to lean on a wall in 33 years of doing this. Surely in those comfy looking Air Jordans, you can stand upright for four 45-minute sets. Next time you want to lean, look at my shoes. Then look at yours. Uh-huh.

2) No fighting with and swearing at one another when there are open mics, no bringing up hassles before the gig—you may bring up grievances after work. If you need to make a note to yourself to remember, it probably wasn't that important. Let it go. Show up at least ten minutes before downbeat. When you are late, we worry that you might be lying in a ditch. Then we begin thinking you had better be.

3) If you don't like your mix, please do not glower and stamp your feet like an angry ewe, but go over nicely at the end of the set and ask the soundman to give you what you need, unless you are getting carpet bombed with feedback, in which case, of course you may ask to have it fixed sooner. Pointing and pouting, covering your ears and refusing to sing are not efficient methods of communication. Speak to him in specifics, i.e., "I need to hear more of my guitar/bass/vocals/8k/kick and snare/what-have-you in my mix." Soundmen love the technical and the specific. It makes them all melty inside. Also, the soundman is not psychic, and amidst all his gear, I have yet to see a crystal ball. Be warned: if you want to sing all breathy like Donovan or John Mayer or Luther Vandross, expect some feedback if you want all those nice crispy highs in your monitor. This is the stage, with live drums and all that, not the studio. And as far as that goes, why do you show up with a thousand dollar guitar, $150 shoes and a $60 mic and a borrowed monitor that looks like it was the state of the art for The Delphonics? Just curious...

PS: I will not bring in mattresses so you can have a ghetto-style vocal isolation booth. Deal. If all this displeases you, part with some ducks and buy in-ears. Do NOT expect great vocal sound from an SM 57, and do not expect me to provide mics, mic stands, monitors, wires, guitar stands. It is not my responsibility. If I DO, it is out of the kindness of my heart. Don't complain about them.

4) On the topic of sound, the soundman is a soundman, not a miracle worker, to paraphrase Dr. McCoy. He is working with gear that is the musical equivalent of the space station Mir, and is doing his best. If you don't like what he has, feel free to bring in your own. Soundman: once people are happy, do not touch the mix or I will break your fingers off. I know I have said this before, and you think it's funny or cute or something, but I mean it this time. This next stuff should go without saying:

5) Nobody should tell another bandmember that his harmonies suck as he sings them. We aren't all blessed with perfect pitch like some of you are.

6) Please do not play lead guitar or lead bass or lead keys or drum solo over the lead vocalist—it is distracting at best, rude at worst. We already know you are talented. And please, please,

7) Don't come in late from a break reeking of that fine Colombian to the point where we all get a contact high just by being on stage with you. You know who you are.

8) If your bandmate is chatting up a lovely lady, don't come up and tell her about his nasty underwear. There are limits to all friendships.

9) Do not bring your private stash of liquor into the club, and then act surprised when the club owner starts "trippin'" about it. Some things just aren't done—white shoes after Labor Day, ketchup on hotdogs, spandex at a wedding, and your own liquor in a bar. And you weren't the one who got your ass really chewed, I was, because, ta-da! I am the supposed "band leader." Welcome to the difference between responsibility and power. Oh, yay. But you know what? He/she has a right to be furious, and we're lucky we weren't all fired on the spot for your bonehead move. Simple math: many bands—and believe it or not, lots of them that are cheaperthan we are—and one liquor license, which they could easily lose over something like your neon-blue can of Bud-Light—I mean, couldn't you at least carry in something they sell in the bar if you have to be that cheap/arrogant/stupid? I am pretty sure even the Beatles would have been fired for pulling a stunt like this. Holy cow. And don't look at me like that. The whole band is mad at you. Yes. They are.

10) And finally, if you come to me and say, "it's me or him," I may liberate both of you from your misery. In any case, you may not be pleased with my choice. You think I'm trippin', try me. If you don't like these rules, there are many fast food joints that may offer you a lovely alternate source of income. If you do not like these rules, we will still love you, but we will miss you. To quote Prince, act your age, not your shoe size. There will probably be a copy of Miss Manners book for each of you involved here as well. If so, there will be a test. Flashcards can be helpful. This is the stage—you know—fun. Not life and death, not the ER, not the streets of Kabul or Fallujah. An atmosphere of general civility and tact and

professionalism is what I seek here. Thank You. And a big P.S. to any wanna-be talent agents out there: You tell me you love the band. You tell me you want to be our agent, you tell me you want to have business cards made up, but you don't know exactly what to put on them. You tell me that you expect 15% of my pay for booking us. Fine. It's the going rate, after all. But then! Then you tell me I need to lose weight and be sexy, because the band will fail if I don't. It's all on me, you say. You tell me that in all the years you have seen the band — playing in very nice venues and being invited back time after time — go figure — that I have never been sexy. Hmm. Really. Okay, see, here's the thing, Mister Wannabe Talent Agent Man — if you want to be a talent agent, then sell the talent. If you haven't got the imagination to sell anything but my "sexy," there is another job description for that, I am just not so sure you want to print it on a business card. Buy a fur coat and a purple hat and some bling, though, you'll want to look the part. There's my 15%.

Last call for alcohol...

Peace out.

Thank you:

    For their incredible wisdom, guidance, patience, and grace, and for teaching me to sing in another language, thank you Julie Paegle, Juan Delgado, Kevin Moffett, and Glen Hirshberg. Thank you, Corinna Vallianatos and James Brown, for your pitch-perfect observations. I will always be grateful to Bryce Campbell, Tim Adell, and Andrea Glebe for seeing a writer when all I saw was a musician who typed.

    The First Cohort: Orlando Ramirez, Sara Hastings, Marsha Schuh, Justin Elgar, Joe Huver, Bryan Henery, Melissa Fowler—thank you for your informing my poetic and sharing your lovely work with me every week, constantly raising the bar and coaxing me on, and for never letting me get away with being pitchy.

    Friends and lovely muses of the highest order: John Perham for his elegance and vision, wit and rigor; Margie Lowe-Francis for radiating dignity, poise and charm, and hopefully letting some rub off on me; Susan Landers for her sharp eye and good humor; Faith Dincolo and Connie Lopez-Hood for showing me how the beautiful harmony arrangements went when I couldn't read the chart; Nikia Chaney, Emily De Vicente, Isabel Quintero, Larry Eby, Eric Atkinson, Carol Anderson, Beth Lucas, Ruth Nolan and Benjamin Brittain, and Anita Thomas for the gifts of beauty, kindness, calm, generosity, camaraderie and inspiration. A debt of gratitude is owed to my students, who teach me more than I could ever teach them.

    Many thanks to my family: My mother, Leilani Grajeda-Higley, for her melodic voice and honesty; My father, Ron Poorbaugh for his quiet strength; My sister, Melinda Decuir, for her affection; Chris Urmston for his limitless patience; my Abuelita, Lucy Grajeda, for believing in me enough to let me tell some of her stories; Derek Urmston, for being a brilliant example of how to quietly create beauty. I will always be grateful to Mary Jane Urmston and my Abuelito, Rudy Grajeda, for gently nudging me forward when I felt clueless, clumsy, and hopeless.

    To the Band: Chris, Kenny "Don't Be Afraid to Enjoy Your Life" Tomlin, Michael McDonald, Tom "It'll Be Great" Steed, Robert "Bullet" Harris, Demetrius Staton, Satoshi Kirisawa, Tsugumi Shikano, and Hitomi Moriya for the music in my soul. I couldn't sing without you.

Elisa Grajeda-Urmston

Acknowledgements:

Grateful Acknowledgment is made to the editors of the following magazines, anthologies, and publications in which these poems have appeared, though sometimes in slightly different forms:

Pacific Review:
    The Wendover/Grady Coefficient
Xicano Poetry Daily:
    Grasshopper,
    La Sirena,
    In an Orange County Bar
Badlands:
    One Percent of What Rattles Around in the Chick Singer's Head
Palabra:
    The Eleventy Seven Anxieties of Being on the Road, Drowned Out by Road Noise

About the Author

Elisa Suzanne Grajeda-Urmston is a college professor, artist, and road-weary musician whose recent poetry and short stories have appeared in Whistling Fire, Xicano Poetry Daily, Badlands, Palabra, Tin Cannon, and The Pacific Review.

A Mexican/British, first-generation American daughter of the Borderlands, she was born in San Bernardino, grew up in San Diego, and now makes her home amidst the coyotes, cottonwoods, and ancient Joshua tree forests on the western edge of the Mojave Desert with her husband Chris, and her dogs. She earned her MFA in creative writing at California State University, San Bernardino. Her poetry inhabits a space between ethnicities and borders, genre and gender, love and loss, glamour and spectacle, drawing from her experiences of thirty years in the music business.

About The Artist

Tamara Adams is a self-taught artist, exhibiting her work in galleries and juried art events in the Pacific Northwest for over twenty years. Her colorful acrylic paintings of women and children and contemporary interpretations of traditional iconography pay tribute to the beauty, mystery and strength of the female spirit. With a wide range of artistic influences, she draws much of her inspiration from mythology, culture, spirituality and religion. The concepts and values reflected in her work are meant to inspire people of all walks of life to a deeper spiritual connection.

Encountering the divine can be as simple as a moment of quiet contemplation and these moments are the theme of Adams' work. While exploring her own beliefs and divine potential through art, writing and healing practices, she's created thousands of sacred images and a powerful vision of women who are truly blessed.

More praise for Sound Check...

There's a bit of a walk from lyrics to poetry and back. It's a rare gift to be able to infuse the beats, rhythm, and meter of music – the pure yet somehow alchemical math of it all – from the instrument to the written page, yet have it read like a song. Elisa Grajeda-Urmston is someone who has managed to do this with passion, focus, and a big heart. We need more of this, now more than ever.

--Rick Elias, Nashville singer, songwriter

The subtitle for the crackling, lightning imminent Sound Check by Elisa Grajeda-Urmston (poet) and Tamara Adams (visual artist) is "A Muscian's Journey in song and verse." Yes this book is that... and so much more. Grajeda-Urmston's taut, tight lines gather to show us the tails of Sirenas, the gutted curves of guitars, the unapologetic deeply feeling warrior flesh of women everywhere – women all guts and glory, who just-might – finally and for all put mudflap silhouettes where they belong... in a different universe, away from the enchanted exhausting midnight roads that have always been ours. This book, beyond its incredible versification, its erudite and inspired poetry, its deeply moving lyrics and its almost unique ability to fathom that "Sadness bigger than a song," is indispensable for any one living west of the Great Divide, for anyone who calls herself (despite it all) American. You've not known the backroads and the service entrances and the grimy yet glamorous performance of stages from Tuba City to Laurel Canyon to Vegas and Doheny... until you've read this, a great poetic epic on the order of Kerouac's Mexico City Blues or Rulfo's Pedro Paramo. Part sleep deprived hallucination, part dream, all Sirena, this book beckons, and lets you ride shot-gun, and even Drive... but when it leaves you, you will never be the same. Read With Caution.

--Julie Sophia Paegle, author of Twelve Clocks

Filename:	soundcheckproof3.doc
Folder:	/Users/nikiachaney/Library/Containers/com.microsoft.Word/Data/Documents
Template:	H:\Donovan\Projects\Manuscript Templates\CreateSpace Templates\Template Documents\CSP5.5X8.5.dot
Title:	CreateSpace Word Templates
Subject:	Manuscript Template
Author:	CreateSpace
Keywords:	Public
Comments:	
Creation Date:	11/25/17 8:32:00 AM
Change Number:	2
Last Saved On:	11/25/17 8:32:00 AM
Last Saved By:	Nikia
Total Editing Time:	1 Minute
Last Printed On:	11/25/17 8:32:00 AM
As of Last Complete Printing	
Number of Pages:	69
Number of Words:	7,609
Number of Characters:	36,267 (approx.)

www.ingramcontent.com/pod-product-compliance
Lightning Source LLC
Chambersburg PA
CBHW041527090426
42736CB00036B/224